I0099462

HEART
THOUGHTS

♥♥♥♥♥♥

"A collection of thoughts and inspirations for maintaining a healthy lifestyle, growing and living in peace."

♥♥♥♥♥♥

Original Copyright of materials © 2005 Angela C.
Williams. All Rights Reserved.

ISBN 978-0-6151-6098-6

No part of this book may be reproduced without
written permission in advance from the publisher
except for brief quotes and credits to publisher.

Contact publisher for additional questions @
claudetteexpressions@yahoo.com

♥♥♥♥♥♥♥

FOREWORD

This book is dedicated in part to my daughter,

Amani. I love you very much. Always

remember, life events will occur daily. Make the

best of them by keeping your head lifted and your

heart softened. I pray you will be able to always

reflect on life in a positive manner. I would also

like to give special dedication to my parents

(Leroy and Pearl) who provided me with spiritual

upbringing which has inspired me to seek the

good. Special thanks to my husband (Anthony),

and my sister (Cargina) for your continuous

support and encouragement.

TABLE OF CONTENTS

♥♥♥

I.

♥*Always Be the Natural You*♥

What does it mean to be the natural you?
Some people believe it is the person they have
seen in their parents or in their rearing. Others
believe it is the person they have become as a
result of life experiences. Regardless of what you
believe it is, the essence of the natural you is what
is inside of you.

What makes you comfortable and uncomfortable? What gives you a sense of belonging? What ignites a passion of your thoughts, feelings, or actions? What inspires a greater sense of well-being or awareness within you? When you are able to answer these questions, you begin to discover the natural you. You are the only person who can truly answer those questions because you are the one with all of the answers.

--What makes you comfortable?--

We have all encountered situations that will increase or decrease our comfort level. Have you ever been with a group of people whether co-workers, friends of a friend, friends of family members, etc. and felt uncomfortable in their presence? These situations tend to thwart our ability to be natural. Instead of acting as we normally would, we often evaluate those people and act according to how we feel they expect us to act. Not only does this keep others from seeing us for who we really are, we create a façade which can build barriers to meaningful relationships. When we allow those around us the opportunity to accept or reject us, we allow ourselves to be natural. Acceptance is easy to appreciate as we all want to be accepted. Rejection, however, is not so easily appreciated. If we learn to appreciate our own disposition, we begin to better understand ourselves, accept ourselves, and learn what we value about ourselves as a result of it.

When we truly understand what we value, we begin to understand our true self and chart the course for happiness and peace. Anyone who decides to accept or reject who we are has some things to learn about him or herself, as we all do, in various stages of our lives. Each person has the right to choose what they will learn about themselves as a result of how they deal with others' dispositions. Acceptance and rejection can be viewed as an opportunity to build upon a genuine relationship. It can spawn a new adventure in this life of continuous learning in respect to how we respond. We have the opportunity to determine how we would like to proceed with our new found revelations from others. We are gifted with that choice. It allows us to decide what we feel from the information we have received. We often feel our best and most comfortable when we are around people we know accept us. Therefore, in order to build upon those relationships in which we are comfortable, we have to allow ourselves to be received. If we are not received, then we have at least given ourselves the opportunity to build upon something genuine.

In addition, we allow ourselves to look beyond the superficial ideology of allowing others to define us. It has wisely been stated; *perception is everything*. When we define ourselves we set ourselves on a path that surpasses the boundaries we encounter with the perception of others. We are the perception. No one is required to second guess our genuine nature. There are far more opportunities for perception to be the reality based on our natural being.

Those who choose to elude their natural self momentarily give up the opportunity. With each opportunity we are provided a gift. The gift we each have is of moments in time. How we decide to utilize it is our choice. When we act in a way that does not come natural, we postpone our ability to be a whole person. When we postpone our ability to be whole, we postpone happiness and peace. Time is on our side. We should utilize

it with the opportunities we encounter everyday.

Reflect on the poem below…

TIME
"A Journey's Friend"

A friend gifted to us all
Given daily with a continuous supply of choices
Waiting for you
Significant occasions, Blessed offerings, Valued
memories
Doors open, Opportunity abundant, Exploration
anew
Meaningful, Rewarding, Special, Momentous
Only you can deliver the reward time brings
Time affords us our journey
Our journey lies in the heart
Our heart has its own desire for meaning within
The desire for meaning within creates the desire to
fulfill
The desire to fulfill is satisfied by the course of our
actions
What will be your journey's course through time?
How will you give it meaning for you?
Create, Cultivate, and Explore your journey's
friend;
Time.
A gift and friend to all

Angela C. Williams ©copyright May 2006

What gives you a sense of belonging?

10

What promotes a greater sense of well-being or

awareness within you?

Everyone wants to feel they belong. When we have a sense of belonging, we have a sense of well-being and awareness within. Whether it is within a family, at work, a volunteer group, a church group, a sports team, or other social setting, the desire to belong is natural. Each of these groups is distinctly different, yet the desire to belong is common for all. Still, each of us has individual reasons for having the need to belong as well as individual concepts that give us that feeling of belonging. When we understand and open ourselves to truth, we begin a path of self-discovery which will ultimately lead to greater awareness within.

So why do we have different reasons for needing to belong? Our reasons for the need to belong can stem from past to present experiences. And since each of us receive information in various ways; we create individual desires which lead to individual needs. Understanding our individual reasons for having the need to belong is crucial to overall understanding of self. Understanding self helps us understand why we react the way we do in certain situations.

One may feel they belong as a result of simply being given the opportunity to be on a committee. Another may feel they belong if they are given the opportunity to participate in a committee although they are not a regular committee member. Still others may only feel they belong if they are an active and regular contributor with consistent roles for a committee. Another may feel they belong if they are simply a member of a church congregation or a regular tithe payer. Another may only feel they belong if they are an active participant in services or outreach missions. Each of these examples are different, yet may produce the same outcome dependent upon one's need. Despite the many examples of things that create a sense of belonging, situations in our lives dictate these feelings. Our job is to determine what it is for us and move forward with that knowledge of self. From there, we learn to appreciate who we are a little more each day on our journey to self discovery.

What ignites a passion of your thoughts, feelings, or actions?

We each have something that ignites a passion within. Sometimes we know what they are and in other situations we have yet to discover them. There are times when excitement about a subject of particular interest causes you to feel exuberant. You enjoy talking about the subject and even research things surrounding it. This is driven by a passion you have for the subject. When we notice our passions, we again can begin to understand who we are. Our passions, whether physical, emotional, or spiritual, help us to understand where we are in life. In turn, we learn to grow and belong to our true passions. In essence, we are living from within.

II.

♥*Make Every Day Great and*

Resolve to be Happy♥

It starts with "you" acknowledging your day as a great one. Treat it as such no matter what occurs. Have you ever felt great and began to wonder why you were feeling so good and start to take yourself down? Or, have you ever started out with a great idea and before you knew it, "possible" thoughts of other people about you and your idea begin to cause your excitement to be squelched before you can even start to write it down? These thoughts can cause a continuous cycle of downward spirals of days or ideas that could have been great ones if you had only believed in yourself. When we feel good or have a great idea, there is a reason. Receive what you have been blessed with and move forward thankfully. Believe that, "all things work together for the good of those who love God and are the called according to His purpose''. When you were born, you were called on for His purpose. Resolving to be happy daily will help you live out God's will and you will overcome obstacles you never even knew were there. There will be times when resolving to be happy in situations may require more than the average amount of faith in order to get through them. The difference in you and those who don't resolve to be happy will be

that you didn't allow certain situations to stunt

your growth by dwelling on them which can keep

you from building your house. Building your

house simply means you are getting to that place

you were meant to be. Keep moving forward.

Reflect on the poem below…

RED SEA ENCOUNTERS

*Ever wonder what most would have done if stuck
at the Red Sea with the army behind?
Would there have been enough belief to even
consider stretching out the rod?
With all of the people following and trusting at
that moment
What really would have been done?
Would the voice of God heard by one alone be
sufficient?
What do we do today?
Look at what everybody else is doing
Try to determine if we fit in enough
Wonder if anyone will have enough faith in us
Start believing if we get a boost from man
Have a boost of confidence until someone
questions us
Have you ever wondered?
Do your day to day challenges get you bent out of
shape?
What are your Red Sea Encounters?
Do you believe?*

Angela C Williams © November 2006

III.

♥Associate With All, but Choose Wisely♥

Some people feel they must not associate themselves with certain types of people in order to maintain their own personalities. This can be true to a certain degree. We must know ourselves to determine how much association is warranted. Still, we must decide how to respond in the presence of those people when we do not have a choice. We should not allow ourselves to become so engulfed in another person's world that we absorb it into our own. However, there is always an opportunity to learn from others. Allow yourself room to be social with different types of people but hold your "friends" dear to your heart. Choose them wisely and know you can trust, lean on and confide in them without worry. Friends accept you as you are and you accept them likewise.

IV.

♥*Choose Your Battles*♥

Ever wonder why some people seem to have an opinion about everything? Why some people just don't want to attempt to understand another's point of view? Why some people don't stop to think about what they are saying before they say it; or after? Some things simply aren't worth fighting or arguing over. If you resolve to live a happy life, don't get caught up in meaningless battles over small things. If it seems to be worth the fight, do your research (if necessary), state the facts and move on. Some people live to argue and they don't want to know the facts; they just want to be right even when they are wrong. A meaningless battle of the brains is vain, but a meeting of the minds is fruitful.

V.

♥*Position Yourself for Success*♥

Remember true success starts on the inside and moves outward. Think of how your daily actions reflect on others. Don't only think of yourself, but be cognizant of how your actions influence others around you. In doing so, people will respect you, long to be like you and want to reward you. Success will come to you and nothing will be impossible for you.

People often have a tendency to lean toward those that make them feel good about themselves. Ever notice how people like to be around funny and outgoing people? The same holds true for those people who make others feel good. Do you know anyone who just loves to be around people that make them feel like crap? Not likely. If you see people in that type of situation, they are generally there because they feel trapped and long inwardly to get away. When you feel good about yourself, it is easier to make others around you feel good about themselves.

The longer one is in the presence of unhappy people who spread their unhappiness on others, the less one will be able to see happiness for themselves. Think of happiness and what is good in your life. When you dwell on the good, you will create more good around you. You will create success around you. Success is in you.

You just have to be willing to live within it.

VI.

♥*Guard Your Spirit*♥

Don't allow untamed hearts to penetrate

the mind, body and soul. The untamed can slowly

drain our spirit and cause us to lose sight of our

goals. We all have warning signals when it comes

to our spirit. There is always that something

telling us to go a different way; do what we said

we were going to do; follow the dreams we set.

Yet, we often allow outside influences to deter us

from original plans. Those influences may be inward thought processes or people we are around. There is an old saying you should not take lightly, "birds of a feather flock together". If you gather with them on a regular basis, you will eventually start to take on their points of view. Don't limit yourself from learning and understanding others, but don't become them. Learn to take in wisely. If it seems you are going in the opposite direction of your previous plans, stop, take heed, and listen. You may need to turn back. If you are no longer aware of your spiritual path, you have lost control of your spirit. It is time to get it back. When we take time to realize where we are heading, we again take control of our lives so we can follow our inward spirit.

VII.

♥Seek Wisdom, Knowledge and Understanding♥

Wisdom is the ability to use the knowledge and understanding you have in a tactful and fulfilling manner. It will allow you to surpass the simplicity of taking knowledge from a text book and applying it to simple activities. It will also allow you to go beyond the simplicity of saying I understand and allow you the ability to wisely apply it to meaningful aspects of life.

When you seek these things, you have already moved to the head of the table. It doesn't matter how much money or fame you have. It is not nearly as valuable for you without wisdom, knowledge and understanding. These keys to life bring about richness. They help bring peace to the disturbed, light in darkness and subtle air where it appears dry and sullen. They can promote a sense of awareness that would otherwise be absorbed materially by those who are unwise and without knowledge and understanding. Is it worth it to be a leader without wisdom? It may only drain you of your respect which could cause others to take advantage of you. Is it worth it to be rich and without knowledge? It may only make you look bad as someone could easily make it known they know more. Is it worth it to be wealthy and have little understanding? It may only cause you

heartache due to relying on someone else to keep

you there. Wisdom, knowledge and understanding

will cause you to stand in peace in all situations.

VIII.

♥Success Does Not Always

Appear as Such♥

Success can be viewed in many forms;

wisdom, knowledge, understanding, power,

position, money, experience, and clothing. Think

on the aforementioned things. Without wisdom,

knowledge, and understanding, you can lose your

money, position and power. Position, power and

money can cause trouble to find you due to the continuous spotlight. Experience is only limited to what you, or in some cases others, have been through. Clothing is only an outward view which can easily deceive. Truly successful men/women prefer wisdom, knowledge and understanding, and may be successful without the glitz and glamour often associated with success. Don't kick the old man or woman in his overalls. He or she may have more to give you than you can ever ask for. A wise and knowledgeable person with understanding and experience is one of the best kinds of people to know.

IX.

♥*Keep Small Issues Small*♥

Don't allow small issues to turn into mountains and cloud your thinking. Often times it is easy to allow little things to worry and anger us to the point we forget how small they really are. We often don't realize how small an issue is until we have something bigger to worry and anger us. Then, those little things become smaller again and not so important. So when things are going well

except for small issues in your life, appreciate it

and your life. Don't try to make the small issues

bigger than they are. Save your energy for the

mountains which are a part of life. You'll be

better able to deal with the mountains when you

have mastered the small hills. Let hills be hills

and mountains be mountains. Let peace reign in

your heart.

X.

♥Expressing True Emotions♥

You should never allow anyone to make you feel guilty about expressing your true feelings. If you have true emotions about something, you should feel comfortable expressing them. If someone makes you feel uncomfortable expressing yourself, stop to evaluate that person to determine if their company or friendship is true.

Negative comments in response to your true emotions do not contribute to your well-being. The worse thing any of us can do to ourselves is harbor negative emotions. These things can lead to high blood pressure, stroke, and high stress levels that can cause a host of health issues. When we express true emotions, we allow ourselves and others to see who we really are. Expression of emotions brings out our true self. When our true self is revealed, we learn a little more about ourselves, others learn a little more about us, and our relationships continue to grow as a result.

Reflect on the poem below...

WORTH THE EFFORT

Despite any other thoughts
Whether there is immediate foresight or not
She/He is always worth the effort
Despite an agreement or disagreement with
thought processes
Emotional needs are not political
She/He is always worth the effort
Despite individual differences
This there always will be

She/He is always worth the effort
Despite any fears of not meeting self expectations
When those fears are challenged
She/He is always worth the effort
If she/he is not worth the effort in or out of season
Then her/his significance is diminutive
If she/he is not worth the effort when issues in life
Magnify her/his emotional needs
Then her/his significance is diminutive
If she/he is not worth the effort when just a little
comfort will do
Then her/his significance is diminutive
One's emotions;
Insignificant?
One's emotions are always worth the effort
Else they are of no significance.

Angela C Williams © September 2004

XI.

♥*Admonish Others Now*♥

When there is someone in your life you
admire or respect, take the time to let them know
it. Many of us value positive feedback from
others.

Unfortunately, the negative feedback is
most often given in lieu of the positive. People
often have a tendency to have wonderful things to

say about others when that person is moving far away or has passed away. If one has had bad experiences with a person in the past, they are no longer as significant and can be buried when they are no longer with us. Why not give people their praise when they deserve it? Admonish and give others their appreciation when you encounter it. Not only will it improve the quality of their life as well as yours, but it could trigger more positive interactions.

XII.

♥Keep Your Expectations at the Right Altitude♥

People often fall prey to high expectations. It is a wonderful thing to have high expectations to continue to reach our goals and obtain success. We must set high expectations in these cases. However, when it comes to dealing with others, we often set our expectations too high and later find it difficult to accept people for who they are. We should keep in mind; people can only give what is inside of them to give. The people we encounter in our lives do not owe us the burden of exceedingly high expectations we have created in our own minds and without cause. The expectations we place on others should not be tainted with desire for more than they are willing or able to offer. We can easily end up becoming unappreciative when we set these types of expectations. It is important to learn to appreciate what others do for you as well as to be content with what you have. Contentment means you can be happy with what you have even if it is less than what someone else has. Happiness is about inward contentment. So keep your expectations centered on the proper things in life. Then you will be able to appreciate more things in life that come your way, which will only lead to more.

XIII.

♥*Evaluate Your Actions*♥

Have you ever noticed how many times you've heard people (or yourself) say, "I wish I hadn't said that."? Or, "I know she wish she didn't say that." Too often, we say and do things before thinking about how it may come across to others. Sometimes, we don't realize how offensive those actions are until we see the other person's face, or simply by the way we feel afterwards. What we do and say determine the type of people we attract in our lives. If we desire to attract certain people, we should learn to understand that type of person and reflect that in our actions, conversation, and what we do. This does not mean we have to change who we are. It simply means, make sure our actions are not offensive by evaluating our thoughts before we offend the people we care about and care about us. Avoid offending others.

XIV.

♥*Evaluate Your Past*

Influences♥

Every person on this earth has past influences. Some of those influences were good and some were not so good. There may come a time when you will have to decide if something someone has said to you is an influence based on negative thoughts or feelings from their past or if it is an influence based on positive growth from their life experiences. When you take time to evaluate a person and try to understand why they do what they do, you can better gauge if you are taking advice that is a result of negative influences. We should ensure influences guide us to a place where we can be better people. If past influences are a hindrance to our positive growth pattern, we should take time to seriously evaluate why it is hindering us, what we can do to get past it, and understand continuous growth is a journey.

XV.

♥*Know Your Limits*♥

You are wise when you are able to reflect on yourself enough to determine what types of things you can and cannot handle despite what others around you do or think. If you evaluate an action and determine it has the potential to set you back from your path of growth (whatever phase of life you are in), know how to say no and pass on the experience. We must know ourselves. If you are not able to handle living happily as a single person AND hang out with married people, then don't hang out with married people. As a part of positive growth, we must know what our own true limits are. If you are unable to comfortably work in certain environments, then don't work in that environment. If you are not able to hang around certain types of people and maintain your own identity, then consider a change in the people you are around. Know your limits.

XVI.

♥*Never Settle in Life*♥

Don't settle for only the best you've ever
had, because the best could be yet to come. Don't
settle only for the best you think you can get,
because that is only a sign of insecurity, which can
stifle your daily growth. Learn to understand
yourself enough to know what your needs are and
aspire to find your best and most positive
(spiritual, mental) connections to help you move

forward in your daily growth. Allow your true potential to flourish. Trust that what is for you is that; for you. Life doesn't settle for us, we settle for it. Make the best of life based on your inward spirit. Your spirit is there to guide you on your journey in growth. You have to keep moving forward. To settle is to stop.

XVII.

♥Quality of Life = Choices

Made♥

Choose to do what is going to benefit you in the long run spiritually, emotionally, mentally, and physically. If you take thought of how your choice will affect these important factors in your life, the quality of your life can be better than you imagined. Unfortunately, many people repeatedly make wrong decisions to the point they don't realize how it is impacting their lives. They live with it continuously making wrong choices. Bad conscience or better yet, no conscience can negatively impact your living. Wrong choices lead to choosing to live with it. Choosing to live with wrong choices tend to create living a difficult life. Your life is available for you to make it the best you can make it. If it is empty, you can fill it. What you fill it with is up to you. You have the privilege to choose. Choices are a privilege and you have ownership of them. Choose to live a quality life by making good choices. Your quality of life is in direct proportion to the choices you make.

Reflect on the poem below:

DO; WISELY

I do what
I DO

You do what
YOU DO

Ultimately, we all have something
TO DO

We choose what we
WILL DO

Where we are in life today
Is a result of what we
DID DO

Choose Today
For Tomorrow
WISELY

Angela C Williams © October 2007

XVIII.

♥Offenses; Address Them or Forget Them♥

If someone offends you and you deem it is not important enough to confront that person about it, consider it unworthy of the stress that comes with continuing to think about it. As a result of personality differences, differences of opinion, and various situations, there will be times others will make comments that offend you.

Avoid spending too much time feeling personally wronged by a comment unless you plan to address it. Otherwise, you risk the ability to maintain a positive rapport with others due to hidden offenses. Address it and move on or forget about it.

XIX.

♥Life Has Continuous Fairy Tales♥

You ever notice how fairy tales always end at the beginning of a life changing event? The Princess married the Prince and lived happily ever after. The kiss woke sleeping beauty, their love began and they lived happily ever after. In reality, we all have fairy tales throughout our lives. Life changing events occur sporadically. We have happy and successful occasions, mediocre days, and unfortunate events. Fairy tales display the positive side of life's events on a grand scale. The positive side also comes in smaller ways after the grand show is done. Despite unfortunate events and mediocre days, we should explore life's happy moments to explore life's fairy tales. Consider the poem I wrote below:

Life Fairy Tales

The hustle of nine to five
Daily breaking through people barriers
Feelings, deadlines, expectations, differences
Where is my fairy tale?

The bustle of after five
Daily regularity of to do lists
Cooking, cleaning, preparing for next day
Where is my fairy tale?

In the middle of it all, she came
Looking in my eyes with the sweetest smile, asking
to replay a simple joy of jumping like a frog
We played; We laughed; We hugged
The freshness of it all was a thankful blessing to
behold
There was my fairy tale

In the middle of it all, he came
Looking in my eyes with love anew, reminding me
of the things we still can do
We talked, we flirted, we reminisced
It was just like the first time
There was my fairy tale

In the middle of it all, they came
Speaking to me with familiar tone and laughter
Reminding me of the things from past to present
Reminiscing about the way things used to be
It was a reunion
There was my fairy tale

In the middle of real life
We Live;
Happily in our moments
Ever After.

Angela C. Williams ©copyright May 2007

Fairy tales are not an ending. They are a

beginning. See them in your life.

www.ingramcontent.com/pod-product-compliance
Lightning Source LLC
Chambersburg PA
CBHW021914040426
42447CB00007B/852